Growing Thinking Kids

By Evelyn Petersen
Illustrated by Barb Tourtillotte

Totline® Publications
A Division of Frank Schaffer Publications, Inc.
Torrance, California

Dedicated with love to my children—Heather, Eric, Karin, and Kristin—and to their children and grandchildren. I hope that you and other readers of this book will always make it a priority to take time to enjoy activities with your children. It is through these experiences that we cherish and honor our childhood memories. It is during these moments that we pass on both our old and new family traditions.
Keep making moments that will last for lifetimes.   *—E. P.*

Managing Editor: Kathleen Cubley
Contributing Editors: Gayle Bittinger, Carol Gnojewski, Susan Hodges, Elizabeth McKinnon, Jean Warren
Copyeditor: Kris Fulsaas
Proofreader: Miriam Bulmer
Editorial Assistant: Durby Peterson
Graphic Designer (Interior): Sarah Ness
Graphic Designer (Cover): Brenda Mann Harrison
Production Manager: Melody Olney

ISBN: 1-57029-103-9

Library of Congress Catalog Card Number 96-61891
Printed in the United States of America
Published by Totline® Publications
Editorial Office: P.O. Box 2250
              Everett, WA 98203
Business Office: 23740 Hawthorne Blvd.
              Torrance, CA 90505

20 19 18 17 16 15 14 13 12 11 10 9 8 7 6 5 4 3 2 1

Introduction

From the moment they are born, children use many kinds of thinking skills as they assimilate and learn from information taken in through their senses. Between ages 3 and 6, children continue to learn through hands-on experiences, refining and polishing their thinking skills through practice, experimentation, and trial and error.

It is important for parents to know that young children are eager to learn and learning all the time, no matter where they are or what they are doing. This is the reason you as parents have so many wonderful opportunities in the early years to be your child's first and most important teacher. *Growing Thinking Kids* will help you take full advantage of these opportunities by presenting you with age-appropriate, enjoyable activities that will assist you in developing and nurturing your child's thinking skills.

Growing Thinking Kids emphasizes the kinds of thinking skills that make the wheels turn in children's heads. Ideas include creating, inventing, constructing, comparing, classifying, and experimenting—the kinds of thinking skills that promote problem solving, or "figuring it out." Best of all, you and your child will be able to do thinking-skill activities as you shop, cook, ride in the car, play outside, wait in line, do household chores, and relax together. All of these ideas are easy to put into practice using materials you probably have on hand.

The skills and attitudes children learn before the age of six are vitally important and affect the years to come. What we want most for children is that they keep loving to discover, learn, think, and solve problems, because the world they inherit will need thinkers, doers, and creative problem solvers. I hope the ideas in *Growing Thinking Kids* will bring your family many hours of fun and learning.

A WORD ABOUT SAFETY: The activities in *Growing Thinking Kids* are appropriate for young children between the ages of 3 and 5. However, keep in mind that if a project calls for using small objects, an adult should supervise at all times to make sure that children do not put the objects in their mouth. It is recommended that you use art materials that are specifically labeled as safe for children unless the materials are to be used only by an adult.

Contents

Thinking Skill-Builders

Thinking Skill-Builders

We live in an age of high technology and we are becoming a global community. Knowing and being able to repeat memorized facts is not enough in today's world. We need to be able to use our thinking skills to work with technology, and we need to use problem-solving skills to work cooperatively on world problems. Because this is the world your young child is entering, we must try to provide every possible opportunity to practice thinking and problem solving.

Fortunately, many opportunities for practicing different types of thinking and problem-solving skills exist every day in your own home. In the course of an average day, you can give your child chances to practice skills such as observing, discussing, predicting, estimating, linking cause and effect, comparing, perceiving, inventing, and discovering. These skills will help prepare your child to be a better reader, scholar, and problem solver. "Thinking Skill-Builders" will help you see ways to use ordinary things or events in your home to help your child build thinking skills.

Learning in Action

Carefully observe your child at play with toys, blocks, or sand and water. After just a short time, you will see him practicing many skills. You will see guessing, estimating, counting, measuring, sorting, matching, and grouping.

You may also see your child practicing comparing and sequencing as he puts toys or play materials in a certain order. When you see your child practice problem-solving skills in play, praise him by giving him words that describe his thinking process. Try using phrases like "You put these in order from smallest to largest," or "You found the ones that match."

When you play with your child, you will see that play is work through which your child learns.

Playing and Thinking

When making decisions each day, children use many problem-solving skills. Daily choices your child might make include what she will play with, who she will play with, where she will play, and how long she will play with a particular item.

Play gives children practice in real problem-solving skills as they make choices, prioritize those choices, and plan their time. Try to see your child's play in this new way and let her make decisions and choices as much as possible, because these decisions will help your child begin to learn basic life skills, such as time management.

Children practice all kinds of problem-solving skills through their play.

What Will Happen?

Estimating and predicting are essential thinking skills and life skills. Estimating and predicting will help your child know how much money he is spending on a shopping trip, how much of a certain material he may need to build something, how long it will take to get from one place to another, and so forth.

The need for estimating and predicting will pop up in your child's life over and over again.

Opportunities to practice estimating or predicting skills abound in your home. Do some exploring with your child. If you take a look around your house you will be amazed at all the different materials you can use to practice estimating and predicting skills. Use the various items you collect to make up games with your child.

For example, guess how long a roll of toilet paper will last. Or, guess how long a pitcher of juice will last. Try setting out a few kitchen gadgets and letting your child guess what they are used for. Then, help him use some of the gadgets to see if his predictions were correct.

What's Inside?

Set out several pieces of fruit, such as an apple, a banana, an orange, and a tomato. Show your child the outside and inside of the fruits and discuss the differences in color and texture. Now, help your child cut a piece of the fruit in half. How is it different on the inside than on the outside? How does it smell? Are there seeds? How many seeds do you think there are? How can you get them out? Can you count the seeds? What do you think should be done with the seeds? Explore the insides of the other fruits. Lots of thinking can be practiced in just a few minutes with one piece of fruit.

This guessing game promotes observation skills.

Observing and Predicting Changes

One of the most interesting things children discover while cooking is that many foods change when they are cooked. Take a few minutes to boil a piece of apple, potato, or carrot. Ask your child to predict what will happen to the food as it cooks. Let your child taste a piece of raw apple, potato, or carrot, and then let him taste the cooked version. Talk about how the food changed in texture, taste, smell, and appearance.

Children practice many thinking skills when they help prepare food.

Observing and Telling

Whenever you get the chance, encourage your child to talk about what she is doing when she plays.

As soon as children become talkers and questioners, they continually practice the first two steps of the scientific method—observing and telling. When you watch your child at play, listen to what she says. You will see that she is continually practicing the science skills of observing and telling. Encourage the use of these skills by prompting your child to observe things and then talk about them wherever you go.

For example, when driving in the car, ask your child what she sees out the window, and then encourage her to describe it. When you are outdoors ask your child to describe a plant or flower to you. Can you guess its identity? Help her observe and tell you the differences between weeds and flowers. Help her observe healthy, ripe, undamaged produce in the store. Help your child observe something nice about someone else and tell them.

Learning About Cause and Effect

Understanding the relationship of cause and effect will help your child be a good problem solver in later life.

As children play, they continuously experiment to see what will happen. They ask themselves questions, try something, and discover their own answers. Will this puzzle piece fit in this space? How many beads can I put on this string? What can I use to fill this bucket? How can I make a house for this doll? Is this too heavy to carry? What if I drop it?

When doing this, your child's learning experience is going deeper than simply learning the answer to the question at hand. By his continuous experimentation, he is learning the natural thinking skill of trial and error, and he is also learning about cause and effect. Praise and encourage his problem solving by describing what he did. Say something like "Great job! You figured out a way to fill the bucket!" Here are two ways to help your child learn more about cause and effect.

Try this fun game together. Set out a vacuum cleaner with a hose attachment and place a paper plate on the floor. Turn on the vacuum cleaner and let your child put the hose on top of the plate. Have him lift the hose into the air. Why is the plate sticking to the end of the hose? Turn off the vacuum cleaner while the hose is still lifted. What happens to the plate? Why?

Plant some grass seed in two margarine containers. Ask your child what he thinks will happen if he waters only one of the containers. Try this for a week to find out. Whenever your child thinks about why something happens, he is learning about cause and effect.

What's Missing?

Challenge your child with this fun memory game.

Most children enjoy using memory skills. They like to sing favorite songs or retell stories they've heard before. When your child becomes an adult, she will often need to recall many small details or sequences of events in order to think through and solve problems, so sharpening memory skills is important. To practice memory skills, try the game that follows.

Collect items that are familiar to your child, such as a comb, a hairbrush, a toy car, a book, a block, a spoon, and a toothbrush. Have your child examine the items and name each one. Ask her to close her eyes while you remove one of the items. Now, have her open her eyes and guess which item is missing. Follow the same procedure with the remaining items. For older children, include more items and change their positions each time you repeat the game.

Following a Line

Learning to walk along a straight line is an important skill that relates to successful reading later on.

When your child learns to read, he will need to be able to follow a line of print with his eyes. Before he can do this with his eyes, he needs to learn to do it with his body. Make or find a straight line (such items as a taped line on the floor, a log, a curb, a wall, or a balance beam work well) and let your child practice walking along it. You give it a try, too. You'll be surprised at how challenging this can be!

Other opportunities to practice working with lines occur during art and outdoor play. When your child uses paint, crayons, markers, or scissors, he makes his arms and hands work with his eyes to follow the lines he makes. Each time your child tosses and catches a ball, he is making his eyes follow a line, even though it is an invisible line. All these things practiced in play will help your child later in following a line of print.

oys

The ability to focus on just one word or a few words on a whole page full of print is a vital skill used when learning to read. When your child learns to read, she will need to be able to see the whole page, but at the same time focus on just one small thing amidst all that background. When children play with puzzles or flannelboard pieces, and even when they do a painting or a collage, they are practicing this skill. They are training their eyes to focus on just one item, but they are still seeing the whole puzzle, design, or picture. Make toys such as puzzles, paints, and collage materials available to your children often.

Toys are integral to a child's development and learning.

Seeing Small Differences

Noticing differences in things your child sees is an important prereading thinking skill he will use in school.

When your child learns to read someday, he will need to notice very fine differences in letters or words that look almost identical. Help your child develop this skill by encouraging him to notice differences in building blocks, beads, puzzle pieces, Legos, and so on as he plays.

When he is dressing, point out the differences in similar items of clothing, or ask him if he notices anything different about similar pairs of shoes. Ask him about differences among similar foods, such as crackers or pasta. Flowers and plants are also good tools to use for observing differences.

Many table games, such as lotto, concentration, or card games, help children train their eyes to see small differences. Encourage your child in play that will help his eyes to see differences. This will help him later when he is learning to read.

Hearing Small Differences

When children play, they are alert to sounds, and they like to identify where those sounds come from.

Children enjoy games that make them guess what sounds are or match sounds to each other. This kind of play trains their ears to hear small differences between sounds.

It is important for your child to practice this skill, because when she learns to read she will need to be able to distinguish the differences between letters that sound almost identical, like *F* and *V* or *B* and *P*.

Try tape-recording different sounds around your home, such as a dog barking, the dishwasher running, the toilet flushing, the vacuum humming, daddy snoring, and so on. Your child will love listening to the tape and naming all of the sounds. Let your child make her own tape of sounds to listen to.

Puzzles, Flannelboards, and Designs

These activities will help your child when he learns to read.

When your child learns to read, he will need to be able to focus on just one word or a few words on a whole pageful of print. When children play with puzzles, make designs with parquetry chips or other manipulatives, work with flannelboard pieces, or even when they paint or make a collage, they are practicing this skill. They are training their eyes to focus on just one piece of a material, but they are still seeing the whole puzzle, design, or picture. Use some of the following ideas to make your child some quick games.

- To make a simple flannelboard, attach a large piece of flannel or felt to a piece of cardboard. Cut simple shapes out of felt and let your child move them around on the board.

- Put together a "design box" by placing such things as yarn pieces, poker chips, colored plastic toothpicks, or bottle caps in a box. Let your child play with the items in the box and create all sorts of designs. Make a collage box in the same way, but include glue or tape as well.

- Use magazine pictures, cardboard, and glue to make your child some simple puzzles.

Take-Aparts

Nothing is so exciting to a child as getting to use real tools to take something apart.

Save those broken appliances, such as telephones, speakers, radios, or VCRs. Find your child some space, give her a short, stubby Phillips screwdriver, and help her get busy!

Foster predicting and estimating skills by asking your child what she thinks a certain part was used for and how she would use it.

Curiosity, discovery, and problem solving all happen when children take things apart and see what is inside. If you don't happen to have any old or broken appliances around your home, try asking an appliance or electronics repair person for a "donation," or go to a thrift shop and find an inexpensive appliance for your child to take apart.

Kids and Computers

Fostering your young child's curiosity in computers will lead to continued interest later in life.

Many parents own personal computers, and most 3- to 5-year-olds are quick to develop a healthy interest in experimenting with them. It's best not to rush your child into using software that "teaches" the alphabet, numbers, colors, or shapes. First, he should experiment with the computer under your guidance to discover simple cause and effect actions such as what happens when he touches the keyboard and when he points and clicks the mouse.

Make computer experiences fun by choosing software that rewards your child for his actions by providing fun sounds and bright colors. Later, let your child help you choose some games that will help him practice concepts, or simple software that interests or excites him. Your librarian can help you choose appropriate software, or he or she can get you in touch with someone who can help you. Also, check your favorite newsstands, bookstores, or supermarkets for family-oriented computer magazines.

Problem-Solving Pointers

Problem solving is a process you can help your child practice throughout out the day.

When faced with a problem, young children need help developing solutions and putting those solutions into action. To young children, problems come in all shapes and sizes. Not being able to move a block tower without making it topple can be just as problematic as having to share a favorite toy with a friend or sibling. When you notice that your child is faced with a problem, try helping her follow the steps listed below to solve it. Along with solving the problem at hand, she will be using and learning all sorts of thinking skills.

1. When you or your child notice a problem, discuss it together. Ask open-ended questions that begin with "What if?" or "Why do you suppose?" to foster critical thinking skills.

2. Encourage your child to think about possible solutions. Listen to and respect all of the ideas. You may even want to keep a record of the solutions suggested in case your child wants to try more than one.

3. Help your child examine the advantages and disadvantages of various solutions and then, together, choose one that seems workable. Let your child know that it's all right to take a guess or try a new idea, even if she isn't sure it will work.

4. Let your child try out the solution she decided upon. Observe carefully to see how you can facilitate the problem-solving process.

5. With your child, discuss whether the solution to the problem was successful. If appropriate, help her think of changes she might want to make, or encourage her to try other solutions.

6. As much as possible, avoid solving your child's problems for her. Trust her to come up with solutions, and then be available to help if needed. Children learn best by doing. Sometimes, you will need to help her understand that there are no "perfect" solutions.

Problem-Solving Opportunities

Your home is filled with wonderful problem-solving opportunities.

To grow thinking kids, take advantage of every possible problem-solving situation; help your child think and "figure things out."

⌗ You and your child are playing outside on a snowy day. When you come inside, your child's hands are cold. What are some ways he can warm them up?

⌗ The nozzle of your child's glue bottle is stopped up. How can he clear the stopper so the glue will flow again?

⌗ Your child is trying to build a tall block tower. Each time the tall tower almost reaches shoulder height, it falls down. How can your child make a tower that doesn't fall down so easily?

⌗ Your child's rubber ball is flat and won't bounce. Are there other ways he can play with it?

⌗ You and your child are having lunch and you have only one sandwich and one apple. How can you and your child share the meal?

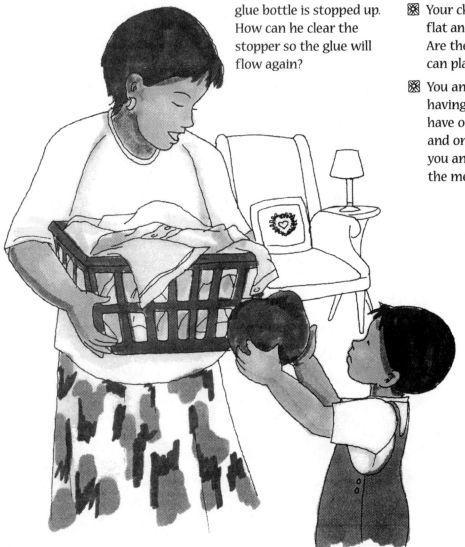

Discovering Similarities and Differences

Discovering Similarities and Differences

During the course of each day, opportunities will arise for you to guide your child in noticing how things are alike and how they are different.

When your child sorts and matches things such as clothing, toys, shapes, silverware, and so on, he is practicing perception skills and learning to differentiate between the characteristics of different objects.

During quiet times, you can give your child cards, poker chips, or household items to sort and match. Ask your child to find the items that are the same and those that are different. Encourage him to tell you the reasons for his sorting or matching choices.

In this chapter, you will find more ideas for giving your child a head start on understanding similarities and differences.

Sorting and Matching

When children sort and match they are also practicing perception skills and learning about things in their environment.

Sorting and matching are the first steps toward grouping and classifying, which are math/science skills. Encourage your child to sort and match at every opportunity you or she can think of. Below are some ideas to get you started.

⊠ Let your child sort some of your costume earrings and put them in matching pairs.

⊠ Let your child sort out magazines by title. (Children can usually do this by looking at the cover pictures.)

⊠ Let your child sort shapes cut out of different colored paper.

⊠ Have your child sort and match big paper clips and small paper clips.

⊠ Set out a container of different types of pasta for your child to sort.

⊠ Let your child separate her storybooks by type or by size, or sort her own books from any library books she has.

⊠ If you have an overloaded button box, have your child sort out the buttons by size or by color, and put each type into small resealable bags. If you help your child notice, she can also sort the buttons according to how many holes are in each one.

⊠ Children love to sort and match bottle caps, so save the caps in a bag or box.

All Around the Kitchen

The kitchen is the perfect place to put science and math thinking skills into action.

Make your kitchen a learning environment for your child by inviting him to help you do certain tasks. Here are some ideas to get you started.

- Encourage your child to help sort groceries. Let him separate the things that don't belong in the kitchen from the other groceries, and the paper goods from the foods. Encourage him to sort meats, fruits, vegetables, cereals, soups, pet foods, breads, and pasta.

- Place forks, table knives, serving spoons, and tea-spoons in a dishpan. After your child washes and dries the silverware, encourage him to sort the pieces into a silverware drawer organizer. Or, let him put the knives, forks, serving spoons, and tea-spoons into separate piles.

- Provide your child with plastic dishes and silver-ware. Show him a correct place setting that includes a plate, a cup, a knife, a fork, and a spoon. Then, ask him to follow the pattern you created to make additional place settings on the table.

- Set aside a drawer in your kitchen for old measuring cups, measuring spoons, bowls, and pans to use for pretend cooking fun. Your child will love "cooking" with dry beans and peas or modeling dough. You may also want to keep a set of picture recipe cards on hand. Try creating a card for a simple no-cook recipe that your child can follow to make a small treat.

Laundry

Laundry provides excellent practice for both sorting and matching.

Each time you do laundry, use it as an opportunity for your child to practice sorting and matching. For example, let her sort all the socks by size and color, finding the matching pairs. Ask your child to sort the washcloths by color and fold them. Then, have her sort underwear and towels by size and type.

Pencils, Pens, and Markers

Your junk drawer gets cleaned while your child practices sorting and matching skills!

If you are like most parents, you have several containers of pens, pencils, and markers, all jumbled together—half of which probably don't even work anymore. Let your child help sort the writing utensils by separating the pencils, pens, and markers into three different containers.

Give your child some scrap paper and let him try each pen, pencil, and marker, and throw away those that don't work.

Stamps and Coupons

Let your child help you save money by sorting coupons.

For one or two months, save all of the stamps from the mail your family receives. (Cutting the stamps off the envelopes is a great job for older children.) Set out several plastic margarine tubs and attach an example of a different stamp to each container. Let your child sort through all of the stamps, placing each design in the appropriate container.

If you save coupons, your child can use the pictures on the coupons to sort them into categories such as cereal, soap, pet food, medicine, soup, and so on.

Make a book for your coupons by using a set of resealable plastic bags that you can put into a small, empty three-ring binder. Punch holes on the bottoms of the bags so that the resealable sides can be opened and shut. This will make it easy for your child to sort and organize the coupons for you to use.

Hardware

Children enjoy sorting nails, screws, bolts, washers, and other small pieces of hardware. Set out several baby food jars and sit with your child while he sorts the hardware.

Keys are a wonderful item for your child to sort into groups. Children will usually start out by sorting keys by size or by color, but as they increase their thinking skills they will look for other attributes of the keys. They will try different ways to sort the keys, such as by shape, or by the size of the holes in them, or even by their use.

For another fun hardware sorting activity, set out a piece of Styrofoam and a Phillips screwdriver (the Phillips is easier for young children to use). Let your child screw and unscrew matching types of screws into the Styrofoam. This activity helps your child practice problem solving, eye-hand coordination, and concentration skills.

Your tool box is perfect for teaching matching and sorting.

Money

Just empty your pockets or coin purse to get the main ingredient for these simple games!

Give your child many experiences sorting and matching real coins. The more she handles and sees the differences in the coins and their money values, the better she will understand the concept of money later in life. Here are some simple ideas for money games. (Be sure your child washes her hands with soap after handling coins.)

- Hide pennies, nickels, or dimes in a sandbox. Let your child have fun finding the "treasures" and then sorting and counting them.

- Write the numerals 1, 5, and 10 in the bottom of the cups in an empty egg carton. Give your child several pennies, nickels, and dimes, and let her toss the coins into the corresponding egg cups.

- Place several pennies, nickels, and dimes in a coin purse. Give the coin purse to your child and ask her to remove the coins one at a time and place them in four separate piles. Then, give your child directions such as: "Put three pennies into the purse. Put one quarter into the purse. Put two dimes into the purse." Now let her give you directions for taking the coins out of the purse and putting them back in.

Setting the Table

Setting the table is the perfect way to introduce the math concept of one-to-one correspondence.

Setting the table is a wonderful way to reinforce one-to-one correspondence skills. Have your child count how many people will be eating. Are there enough chairs for the people? Put out the plates, one at each place. Ask him to count the plates, and then show him that there is the same number of plates, chairs, and people. Continue this process with the cups, napkins, and silverware. Every time your child sets the table, he is practicing thinking skills.

Try some of these other fun activities learning one-to-one correspondence: matching feet to boots, mittens to hands, hats to heads, buttons to buttonholes, cookies to children, pegs to holes, and so on.

When your child does these kinds of activities often enough, he will begin to understand that numerals match sets of actual objects that he can count.

Learning About Sets and Groups

Counting sets and groups is an important foundation for addition and subtraction.

Children need lots of experience counting real things before they understand that one is a quantity of one; two is a set of two that is more than one; three is a set of three that is more than two, and so on.

Give your child many sets of different objects to count. At first, keep the quantities between one and five objects. When your child becomes more adept at counting sets, increase the number of objects. Good objects for counting include buttons, marbles, blocks, bottle caps, keys, paper clips, spoons, forks, and so on.

Help your child see groups or sets in everyday life. Aquariums provide a wonderful set-counting opportunity. Point out that there is a whole group of many fish. Ask your child if the fish can be grouped differently (by color, type, or size, for example).

If you have plants in your home, ask your child to count how many you have altogether, and then break them into groups. For example, some may be flowering plants and some may not—two groups. Using everyday objects your child is familiar with makes her learning meaningful, memorable, and fun!

Playing Cards

A deck of cards is a wonderful tool for practicing thinking skills.

There are many ways for your child to use old decks of playing cards to practice thinking skills. First, your child can practice sorting all of the cards into two groups by color. Teach your child what hearts, diamonds, spades, and clubs look like, and then let him sort the groups of colors into groups of suits. Next, your child can separate the face cards from the number cards.

Now, you can show your child a new way to sort and match—by the type of card. Help him discover that he can make groups for each kind of face card and each kind of number card. Each of these groups of cards will contain two colors and four shapes. Play simple card games with your child to practice sorting, matching, and recognizing numerals.

Homemade Card Games

Make your own games by drawing on index cards or by gluing cut-out magazine pictures on the cards.

Card games are easy to make. All you need is a pack of index cards, markers, old magazines or catalogs, a pair of scissors, and some glue. Following are some ideas for making matching, sorting, and "one of these things is not like the other" games.

⊠ Make eight cards showing four pairs of identical animals. Mix up the cards and let your child find the pairs. You can also make a set of sorting cards with zoo animals, circus animals, and ocean animals. Try making a set of cards showing mother and baby animals.

⊠ Draw apples on four cards, showing one that is yellow and three that are red. Which one doesn't belong?

⊠ Make a set of cards with fruits on them and a set of cards with vegetables on them. Let your child sort them by color, shape, or fruit versus vegetable.

⊠ Cut pictures from magazines to show ways to travel over land, and slip in a card that shows a boat. Which does not belong?

⊠ Make some card games that show sets of different shapes, numbers, or upper- and lower-case letters. Let your child match the pairs.

Understanding Relationships

Understanding Relationships

The more children understand relationships among the things that surround them in their daily lives, the more they can learn about our world and the way it works. Even very young children can begin classifying objects such as parents and children, fruits and vegetables, and play clothes versus dress-up clothes.

This chapter provides you with ideas for guiding your child in activities that will help her understand relationships between objects, how opposites relate to each other, and spatial relationships.

Understanding relationships among things will help your child as she gets ready to read, write, add, and subtract. These ideas will help you give your child a head start comprehending concepts she will learn later in school.

Alike and Different

Throughout the day, encourage your child to think about things that are alike and different.

Everywhere you go, search for opportunities to point out things that are alike and things that are different. For example, when you are in the car, ask your child to notice all of the red cars, blue cars, trucks, or vans. When children use one attribute to find things that are alike, they are practicing perception as well as learning about relationships.

There are many table games available that help children practice sorting and matching by similarities and differences, but it is more fun to start by using everyday things. Use stones, shells, socks, coins, potatoes, fruits and vegetables, and so on.

Collecting

Collecting is a wonderful first step to classifying and understanding relationships.

Introduce your child to collecting by talking with her about collecting and showing her some of your collections, if you have any. If you don't have a collection, ask neighbors or friends to share theirs with you and your child. They may collect stamps, teacups, sports cards, or dolls, for example. Encourage your child to notice all of the different types of things that fit into one large collection.

Museums are a great place to reinforce the concept of collections. If your town has a transportation, natural history, or children's museum, visit it with your child for a couple of hours. Point out all the different types of collections in the exhibits, such as dinosaurs or rocks.

Here are some collecting ideas for you and your child to try.

* Help your child start a collection of her own. Some ideas for fun collections are magnets, toy cars, stickers, shells, marbles, postage stamps, buttons, or rocks.

* Let your child keep her collection in an empty egg carton. She may want to decorate her carton with magazine pictures of items from her collection, or with paint or markers.

* Give your child a paper bag and take her on a collection walk. As you stroll, encourage her to pick up such things as small rocks, leaves, twigs, and bits of moss. When you get home, help your child arrange her nature collection in an empty egg carton or other container.

Observing

Observing and then sharing those observations is a skill that your child has probably already mastered!

Observation skills play a large role in understanding relationships. In order to decide how things fit together, your child needs to observe those things and decide upon common attributes. To practice observation skills, try this fun activity. Go for a walk and help your child observe the signs of the season. If it's fall, he may notice people wearing warm clothes, raking leaves, or chopping wood. He may see birds flying south, animals gathering or storing food, or colorful leaves. Encourage him to name all of the seasonal signs he sees.

Let your child choose a few leaves off of the ground and make a souvenir leaf collage. Encourage him to use fall colors on his collage.

Here are two more ideas for you to use to help your child become more observant.

⊠ Give your child two similar objects to observe, such as two pieces of fruit, two toys, or two books. Ask him to carefully look at the objects, and then tell you how the objects are alike and how they are different.

⊠ For a different observation experience, let your child look through a broken camera or one without film. Let him look through the viewfinder and describe what he sees.

Classifying Fun

When children sort, match, and put things into groups, they are beginning to classify things according to one common attribute.

As children practice classifying, they become very skillful at grouping things in different ways. They may sort and group items by color, size, or shape, or by smoothness or roughness, by smell, or by the ways the items are used. To foster your child's classifying skills, try some of the following ideas together.

※ When doing errands together, encourage your child to notice the different cars in a parking lot. What are some of the ways to group the cars? If there are trucks in the lot, do these belong in the group of cars or not?

※ Give your child a muffin tin or egg carton and set out a pile of bottle caps, buttons, shells, small rocks, coins, etc. Let your child choose some categories and classify all of the objects in the pile.

※ When out on a walk together, gather several different types of fallen leaves. Let your child classify the leaves when you return home. She may decide to group by shape, by color, by type, or by size.

※ Turn cleanup time into classifying time. Label your child's shelves and containers with the pictures and names of the items stored on and in them. Help your child sort the items to put away. Your child will love this activity, and cleanup time will be much easier for you!

What's In My Purse?

This classifying game is fun to play while waiting in a doctor's office or while traveling.

Help your child practice classifying skills by playing a simple game with items from your purse, pocket, or wallet. Lay out a variety of objects, such as keys, a lipstick, a pen, a pencil, some coins, a plastic travel toothbrush, a credit card, and so on.

Ask your child, "What are some different ways we could put some of these things together?" Be aware that a 3-year-old will find only a few ways and may just want to handle the items because she may see the whole group as "things that are my mom's or dad's." Show him that the items might be grouped by big things and small things, or by general color or shape.

A 4- or 5-year-old will find many ways to group the items: by color, shape, size, what they are made out of, how they sound, and how they are used, for example.

Opposites

The concept of opposites can be learned through your child's five senses.

Young children are naturally curious about the similarities and differences they notice between things in their environment. To take advantage of this interest, provide your child with lots of opportunities to practice opposites, which is an important math, science, problem solving, and reasoning skill. Here are some ideas to get you started.

※ Collect boxes of various kinds. Set the boxes out and let your child explore all of the opposites she can find. For example, encourage her to notice big and little boxes, open and closed boxes, light and heavy boxes, thick and thin boxes, full and empty boxes, and wide and narrow boxes.

※ In a bag, place several objects that are hard (a wooden block, a metal spoon, a rock, etc.) and objects that are soft (a cotton ball, a small stuffed animal, a woolen sock, etc.). Let your child remove the objects one at a time and sort them into two piles—one for hard objects and one for soft objects.

※ Set out a box of fabric squares. Let your child rub her hands over each square and decide whether it is rough or smooth. Then have her sort the squares into two piles according to texture.

※ To explore cool and warm, serve your child a cup of warm cocoa, then a glass of chocolate milk. Talk about the difference in the temperature. Does the temperature make the drinks taste different?

Spatial Relationships

If you've ever looked through bifocal glasses or misjudged something and bumped into it, you'll appreciate the importance of this concept.

Spatial skills are learned rather than instinctive skills. When your child first began to crawl, he was learning to perceive and judge distances between himself and the things around him. As he began to walk, run, and climb, he was learning to judge how he should move in order to avoid colliding with the things in his environment. Even now, your child is continually working to avoid obstacles and practice the ways his body moves through the space around him.

Just as children learn spatial skills in relationship to their bodies, they learn how objects relate to each other spatially, including numbers, letters, words, and eventually sentences. Some children master the intricacies of spatial relationships earlier than others, and occasionally a child will constantly be working on this skill, even as he grows into adulthood.

Spatial Relationship Games

You and your child will love these fun games!

Use two small rugs or carpet squares to play "Do What I Do" with your child. Lay the rugs on the ground and give your child movement suggestions such as walking around the rug, jumping over the rug, standing next to the rug, standing behind the rug, and putting your feet on the rug. Try giving some silly suggestions such as sitting under the rug. Let your child give suggestions, too.

Another spatial relationship game is "I See Something." Start the game by silently choosing an object that you see nearby, such as a ball. Give a clue such as "I see something in a corner that is fun to play with." Have your child try to guess what the object is. Continue giving clues that describe the object's position until your child guesses the object.

Fun With Position and Direction Words

Knowing what position and direction words mean will help your child understand directions when he goes to school.

Understanding position and direction words is crucial to understanding relationships. Your child will need to know these words when he starts school. He will be asked to do many things such as go to the *front* or *back* of the room, stand in the *middle* of the line, walk *beside* a certain person, stand *next to* a person or object, go *around a corner* to the drinking fountain, and so on.

To introduce your child to these words, simply integrate them into your daily activities. One of the easiest ways to do this is to ask your child to describe the location of an object. Help him by asking him questions using the position words, such as "What is the juice sitting next to? Is the toy on the top shelf?"

Other ideas include pointing out your position in a grocery-store line or practicing front and back by asking your child to point to the fronts and backs of his stuffed animals. Make up a game where your child walks in a straight line and you give him directions to walk forward, backward, or sideways.

When playing with blocks, encourage your child to build a tower and then name the color of the block on the bottom, on the top, and in the middle. Line up several of your child's toys and ask him to name the toy sitting next to or beside the teddy bear, for example. Your child will enjoy these games, and he'll soon start using position words without your prompting.

Putting Things in Order

Putting Things In Order

Putting things in order is a natural human characteristic. We can put things in order by size, by order of events, and by number amounts, just to name a few methods.

Counting and naming what happens first, second, and third are two of the most basic ways of putting things in order. This chapter covers many types of ordering, including numbering, sequencing, patterning, and other exciting ways to put things in order.

The more opportunities you give your child to hear words and phrases about putting things in order and the more you give concrete examples of their meanings, the more skills your child will process.

You and your child will enjoy these easy, fun activities designed to foster your child's ordering skills.

The Language of Numbers

Talking about numbers with young children makes math part of their lives.

Make numbers and math come alive for your child by integrating them into the way you talk to him. Throughout the day, there are endless opportunities to introduce numbers and math simply by using "math language." Fill your child's world with words, questions, and phrases such as: how many, what next, will it fit, biggest and smallest, taller and shorter, next to, more than and less than, half, whole, names of numerals, and so on.

In the morning, use statements such as "Let's have breakfast first this morning, and next we'll brush our teeth." At breakfast, use different-sized bowls and ask your child if he thinks the same amount of cereal will fit in each bowl.

When you can, let your child help you prepare meals and snacks. Talk about what you are doing, for example, "We need some carrots. Will you count out three carrots for each of us?" "How can we both share this sandwich?" and so on.

Incorporate storybooks with math and number themes into your child's life. There are many choices, and your librarian can recommend the perfect titles for your child's age.

Involve your child in shopping by asking him to find numbers in prices on the shelves, asking him to count certain items, and letting him count coins and pay for things when appropriate. When you are out and about with your child, point out numerals when you see them on road signs or billboards. When at a restaurant, give your child a menu and ask him to find certain numerals.

Incorporating number language into your daily activities and, most of all, showing your child that you enjoy and are interested in numbers and math concepts will help curb the math anxiety that is so common during the school years.

Counting Fun

Your child will love these challenging counting ideas!

Counting is an activity most young children love. If you encourage your child to count at home, you will notice that she will soon find things to count wherever she goes. Here are some easy counting ideas to get you and your child started.

Throughout the day, give your child opportunities to count things. For example, she can count crayons, silverware, chairs, books, toys, balls, coins, shoes, cups, etc. Let her look out a window in your home and count how many cars pass, how many birds she sees, how many trees she sees, how many people pass, and so on. Open the refrigerator and let your child count the items on each shelf or in the door.

Start collecting small items such as buttons, bottle caps, paper clips, nails, and so on. Place them in jars and let your child count them. Give your child some yarn and a pile of large macaroni. Let her string the macaroni to make a necklace and count the pieces as she strings. Can your child find other things around your home to count?

Ordering Ideas

Opportunities for ordering are waiting all around your home!

Many different areas fall under the thinking skill of ordering. The concepts of height, length, size, and sequencing are a few. Here are some interesting activities to help your child practice ordering.

※ Set out three or four cans of different heights. Invite your child to arrange the cans in order of height from shortest to tallest. Add more cans as his abilities increase. You can also make a nesting game from the cans. (Remember to tape any sharp edges.)

※ Give your child lots of practice arranging objects by length. Provide items such as twigs, pencils, pens, yarn pieces, and cut-up straws.

※ Gather some stones outdoors and ask your child to arrange them by weight, lightest to heaviest. Make this easy by choosing stones that are very different weights.

※ Find five empty glass soda bottles and fill them with varying amounts of water. Let your child use a spoon to strike the bottles gently and hear different pitches. (The less water, the higher the pitch.) Ask your child to arrange the bottles from highest to lowest pitch.

Following a Sequence

One of the most meaningful ways to reinforce the concept of sequencing is with pictures of real things and real events that are familiar to your child.

You can easily make sets of sequence cards for just about any everyday or family event. Simply draw each step on a separate index card, or find pictures in magazines to illustrate the steps. You could make sets of sequence cards for getting dressed, making toast or a sandwich, preparing breakfast cereal, or getting ready for bed. Set out any set of cards and have your child put them in order of what happens first, next, etc.

To make extra-special sequence cards, find or take photographs of your child doing a step-by-step activity (helping wash dishes, getting ready for bed, or a family event). Sequence cards with photos of trimming the Christmas tree or giving the dog a bath would be terrific.

Sequence story cards are also easy to make. Select one of your child's favorite stories and divide the story into five or six events. Draw simple pictures of each event on index cards. Use the cards to tell the story; then mix them up and let your child put them in order and tell you the story.

First, Second, and Third

There are many opportunities in your child's environment to practice this ordering skill.

Always try to use real things to talk about first, second, and third, or first, next, and last. Whenever you can, comment on the first person or the last person to get into the car, or the first or last person to brush his teeth. Talk about who is first, second, or third in a line. When stopped at a red light, point out which car is first, second, and third in line.

To foster other ways of understanding ordering, try some of the following ideas. Ask your child to compare the sizes of fruits, vegetables, glasses, balls, nesting cups, measuring spoons, and so on, and then, if possible, place those things in order by size, largest to smallest.

As your child becomes interested, help him put things in order by length (such as sticks or pencils), height (such as bottles or block towers), size (such as bowls, clothes, or shoes), weight (such as stones), and color (such as many shades of the same color—pale pink to dark red).

Following a Recipe

Following recipes incorporates sensory experiences with sequencing practice.

To begin, make a simple recipe chart like the one shown in the illustration below. Set out the necessary ingredients, measuring utensils, dishes, and eating utensils. Show your child the chart and explain the steps. Then let her follow the chart to make the recipe.

Frogs on a slippery log

① 1 banana, peeled

② Spread on — Peanut Butter

③ Top with chocolate chips

Yumm!

Noticing Patterns

Patterning games are especially meaningful because you do them together.

If your child understands the basic concepts behind patterning, he will be better able to anticipate the patterns that will exist in all aspects of his later life. Patterning is a foundation for successful math, science, language, reading, and writing skills.

There are many simple patterning games you and your child can play together. A box of poker chips or a set of checkers is all you need to get started. Sit with your child on the floor or at a table and line up several of the chips in a pattern such as red–white–red–white. Ask your child to copy your pattern. Continue with more patterns, each time making them more complex. Let your child create patterns for you to follow, too.

Encourage your child to notice the patterns that exist in your home. Point out different patterns on rugs, fabric squares, articles of clothing, plates, gift wrap, and so on. Let your child find some more patterns around your home or outside in your yard. Are there patterns in windows or in the garden?

Giving Things Value

Giving Things Value

Young children can't think and figure out in the abstract or "in their heads." They need to experience things through their five senses to understand concepts such as small, big, more, less, light, and heavy.

During your average day with your child, there are natural opportunities to observe how we give things value. We give values to things by assigning numbers, weight, or height. We also measure time and give values to coins and paper money.

This chapter is full of hands-on experiences for you to do with your child to help her begin to understand how we give things value.

Number Values

Number values is a challenging concept your child will enjoy exploring.

Young children know the words *one, two, three, four,* and *five,* but they usually don't understand that two is a quantity that is more than one, or that five poker chips are the same quantity whether they are piled up or spread out.

They need to learn with hands-on experiences that four things have a certain "fourness" that does not change, whether this is four balls, four dots of paint, or four people.

Children learn these concepts gradually, by counting, measuring, matching, sorting, comparing, weighing, and arranging as they play with real things.

As you go through your day together, take advantage of the things that happen and point out different number values. For example, ask your child to find four groups of four at the playground. He may choose to count four children, four swings, and four trees. Or, ask him to count out two of each thing you are having for lunch (carrots, sandwich halves, and cookies).

Set out pennies and have your child make rows and piles that contain five pennies each. Point out that even though the piles and rows look different, the number values are still the same—there are still five pennies in each pile or row.

Money to Spend

Your child will learn about money values by making simple shopping choices.

Let your child do some real shopping. Give her an amount of money that will pay for one of the things on your shopping list, such as a box of cereal. When you get to the cereal aisle, give your child two or three choices of cereal she can choose from. Let her choose the cereal, take it off the shelf, and place it in the basket. If the grocery store has child-sized baskets, let your child place the item in her own basket.

Let your child pay for the item at the checkstand and carry it in the shopping bag. Your child will take pride in her purchase and enjoy eating "her" cereal.

When your child is older, you may want to show her that the weight or size of a product may affect her decision. For example, a larger bottle of juice may be a better buy than a smaller bottle, or a generic cereal may be a smarter money choice than the name brand.

Playing Store

Each time children play store, they use their imagination and practice language, memory, sorting, matching, and number skills.

To set up a play store, use an out-of-the-way corner of your kitchen or another room. Set out a variety of cans or packages of food from your kitchen cupboards. (Or, save containers after you have eaten the food and set them aside for your child's store.)

Help your child make signs to show the name of the store, the prices, and "specials." Set out baskets, used grocery sacks, and an egg carton or muffin tin to use as a cash register. Let your child use play money you've made or borrowed from a board game or, better still, set out real coins.

The wonderful thing about playing store is that you already have all sorts of "merchandise" in your home. If you don't want to set up a grocery store, try a shoe store, a jewelry store, a clothing store, a toy store, etc. Your child will love using his stuffed animals to set up a pet store.

Pet Store

Beginning Addition and Subtraction

4½ and 5-year-olds will love these games.

Even though most children under 7 don't truly understand the big-picture meaning of addition and subtraction, it's not too early to introduce 4½- and 5-year-olds to these concepts. Your child will enjoy the built-for-success beginning games that follow.

Place five identical objects, such as unsharpened pencils, in front of your child. Ask her to close her eyes while you add or remove one to three of the pencils. Have her open her eyes, then help her figure out how many pencils you added or removed.

To help your child learn how to subtract by ones, practice counting backward from 5 or 10 together. For extra fun, call out "Blast off!" each time you reach zero.

Count with your child from 1 to 10. Then ask questions such as: "What number comes before 2? What number comes before 7? What number comes after 3 and before 5?"

Weight and Balance

Your child will enjoy experimenting with the concepts of weight and balance.

Making mobiles and riding on a seesaw are two wonderful ways to help your child learn about weight and balance. To play other games that practice these concepts, it is helpful to purchase a balance scale. Or, make one by attaching plastic cups to either side of a sturdy clothes hanger. By experimenting with the scale, your child will find that sets of the same quantity of the same item (marbles, small blocks, toy cars) weigh the same amount.

As your child experiments with the scale, he will enjoy discovering some surprises, such as some things that are very large (an empty box or balloon) are lighter than something small like a small rock or a magnet. You can also let your child have fun weighing himself and a few of his toys on your bathroom scale.

If you don't have a scale, try this simple activity. Collect four empty margarine tubs that are the same size. Fill each tub with a different kind of material (sand, rocks, cotton balls, etc.), making sure that one of the tubs is noticeably lighter. Tape the tubs closed. Let your child lift each of the tubs and see if he can identify the heaviest and lightest tubs.

Measuring Fun

Your child will love finding different things to measure.

Measuring is especially fun to teach because there are so many ways to experience it. Height, weight, and volume all fall under the skill of measuring, and young children are always interested in these concepts. Try some of the following measuring activities, and then encourage your child to find other objects, and ways, to measure.

- Pour about 3 inches of rice into a plastic dishtub. Set out some measuring tools, such as measuring cups and spoons, and let your child use the tools and the rice to explore measuring concepts.

- Set out a kitchen scale, if you have one, and a variety of fruits and vegetables such as apples, potatoes, carrots, oranges, onions, and bananas. Let your child weigh each item, and then help her arrange the items from heaviest to lightest.

- Hang a growth chart on a wall. Show your child how you will use the growth chart to keep track of how tall she is getting each month. Let your child weigh herself each time you record her height, then add her weight to the growth chart as well.

- Cut pieces of yarn the length of various objects in your living room (a lamp, a table, the TV, a chair, and so on). Give the yarn pieces to your child one at a time, and help her discover which yarn pieces match which objects.

Measuring the Temperature

Your child will be fascinated with these experiments.

Introduce your child to the concept of measuring the temperature by showing him a thermometer and discussing how it is used to measure heat and cold. Demonstrate this by placing the thermometer in warm water, and then in cold water, or in your freezer, and then in room-temperature air.

Have your child watch as the mercury rises and falls. Follow up by letting him measure the temperature of other substances such as milk, soup, or crushed ice. As you talk about temperature, use terms such as *hot, cold, warm, cool,* and *degree.*

Talk about times when your child has been hot or cold, such as during a very hot day during the summer, while standing in the wind, or when he was sick.

Learning About Time

Understanding about the passage of time is another kind of thinking and reasoning skill.

Introduce young children to the concept of time by simply talking about yesterday, today, tomorrow, school or work days, and weekend days. Make your child aware of the time she wakes up, eats, goes places, and goes to bed. Casually tell your child what time it is when each of these events takes place, and show her on a real or pretend nondigital clock. Using a clock when talking about time helps your child begin to associate one with the other. Below are two more ideas for introducing a sense of time to your child.

Make a simple clock out of a paper plate, a paper fastener, and two construction paper "hands." Talk about times of daily events such as lunchtime, dinnertime, and bedtime. Help your child move the hands around the clock to indicate each special time of day.

Set the paper-plate clock for a time when you will do something special, such as reading together. Have your child watch for the matching time to appear on a real clock.

Calendar Fun

To help your child visually comprehend the passage of days, weeks, and months, give him a calendar of his own. Help him place stickers on the holidays or other special days. Each night before bed, let him cross out the square for that day. Knowing that each square on the grid of a calendar equals one day is enough at the beginning. Help your child use the stickers as clues to remember a past event or look forward to a future one. As he grows older, you can begin to discuss the numerals on the calendar or the days of the week.

Other calendar activities include talking a little about what you and your child did yesterday, today, and what you may do tomorrow, while pointing to these days on the calendar. When children have a visual representation of the passage of time, it is much easier for them to understand. Let your child write (or dictate to you) whatever he wishes in his calendar, and save the calendars from year to year. He'll love looking back to see what he did when he was a little boy.

Another fun way to reinforce the concept of passing time is to make a chain calendar together. Simply cut construction paper into 1-inch strips and make a chain by taping the loops together so that they interlock with each other. For each day, add or remove one of the loops. When the last loop is added or removed, the week or month is over, or the holiday or special day has arrived.

Help your child understand the passage of days while creating lifelong keepsakes.

Thinking Skills in Action

Thinking Skills in Action

By now you have realized that your child uses many of the problem-solving skills that have been described in *Growing Thinking Kids* during the normal routines of her day. You have also learned many ways to reinforce and improve your child's skills. In this chapter, you will find even more ideas for taking full advantage of teachable moments with your child. Included are a variety of activities for you and your child to do together. Some activities can be done on the go, some are exciting experiments your child will love, and some are just for fun.

Remember that you can practice thinking skills with your child at any time. Just look around for problem-solving opportunities wherever you are. When you encourage your child's curiosity, thinking processes, and experimentation, you are growing a thinking kid!

Thinking Games

Here are some ideas for quick and easy thinking-skills games to play with your child.

Your child will love playing these simple games, and so will you.

※ Name four things, such as a cow, a pig, a chicken, and a bicycle, and ask your child to tell you which thing doesn't belong in the group. Other ideas for groups include: a bus, a car, a pencil, and a train; a spoon, a plate, a shoe, and a cup.

※ Set out a group of five or so potatoes and let your child choose one. Ask him to study his potato with his eyes and hands, observing and feeling all of the bumps and dents. After one or two minutes, mix his potato with the others and ask him to find it and explain how he knows it is his. Your child's keen observation of detail will amaze you.

※ Find a group of like objects, such as different-colored toy cars. Place three of the cars in front of your child. Have him close his eyes while you remove one of the cars. Now let him open his eyes and tell you which car is missing. As your child becomes familiar with the game, begin each round with a larger number of cars.

Telephone Fun

Inventions of any kind fascinate young children.

When children "invent" something and then try it, they are practicing science and problem-solving skills. If you have an old telephone, give your child a unique thinking-skills activity by helping her take it apart. As she works, talk about what some of the parts are. Ask her what she thinks the parts are used for. It doesn't matter if she's right; the important thing is that she is thinking and "figuring out."

After taking apart the telephone, your child might like to learn how to make a simple telephone, one that you may have made as a child. Find two empty cans and poke a hole in the bottom of each one. Attach a long strand of fishing line (this works better than string) to the cans by threading the line through the holes and securing the ends with a knot tied to a small washer or nut. Now stand far apart to talk to and listen to each other, using your child's new telephone.

Miniature Terrariums

Your child will love making and planting his own terrarium.

This activity is great for practicing predicting and observation skills. To get started, clean out an empty tuna can, then let your child paint over the label. Help your child place a thin layer of small stones and sand in the bottom of the tuna can, then add an inch or so of potting soil.

Now find some clean glass jars. Let your child turn each jar over and set it into the tuna can, trying to find one that fits snugly. Let your child discover which type will fit best. Pint jars will be a bit too loose, but many pickle jars or peanut butter jars will fit nicely.

Let your child place a plant, some moss, and a pretty stone or shell in the tuna can and water the soil just until it is damp. Cover the tuna can with the glass jar and place it in a warm area. Talk to your child about what he thinks will happen to the plant in the jar. Let him observe the terrarium for several days until condensation forms on the inside of the jar. Explain that this moisture will give the plant enough water to live. (This project makes a wonderful gift!)

Junk Creations

Don't throw away all of your junk! Save it for creative thinking skills practice for your child.

If you have toothpicks and some old, stale marshmallows in the kitchen, take a few minutes to sit with your young child to do some creating. Help her connect the marshmallows with toothpicks to make interesting three-dimensional structures. Even a 3-year-old will learn a lot about balance and problem solving from this activity.

Younger children, as well as 4- or 5-year-olds, will also enjoy constructions made of small pieces of scrap wood. Sand the edges if necessary. You can get free scraps from many picture framing shops. All your child needs is a flat piece of wood or thick cardboard to use as a base, and some white glue.

You and your child can also construct three-dimensional junk creations with masking tape and throwaways like paper plates, cups, straws, lids, and toilet paper tubes.

Whenever your child makes inventions or constructions of any kind, she is practicing creative thinking, eye-hand coordination, balance, and problem-solving skills.

Discovery Crawl

Lots of parents take children on discovery walks, but why not try something new—a discovery crawl in your own kitchen or living room. Give your child a paper lunch bag, a small flashlight, and a magnifying glass, if you have one. Let him explore the floor and corners, and place the items he finds in his bag.

When your child is through, ask him questions about each item, such as "What do you think it is? How do you think it could have gotten there? What could it be used for?"

If you want to teach a safety lesson at the same time, place a few items (an empty pill box or empty book of matches) in the room. When your child finishes his crawl, sit with him and talk about his discoveries. Ask questions such as "What if you found this and it had matches (or pills) in it? What should you do?"

Try this activity for an eye-opening experience!

Sleds, Scoops, and Stilts

Use thinking skills to invent new uses for ordinary things!

Encourage your child to think about new ways to use everyday objects. For example, show your child how she can use just about anything slippery to slide on the snow, such as an inner tube, a plastic tablecloth, or a garbage bag.

Another fun thing to do is invent funnels (or a sand scooper and buckets) from 1-gallon milk jugs. Cut the jugs apart at an angle so that the handle end will be the funnel or scooper and the rest of the jug will be the bucket.

Save two sturdy empty cans (paint cans are strong), and drill two large holes in each of them, one on each side, near the top. Have your child help measure a piece of rope "her size" and string it through the holes, knotting the ends. (Measure the rope by looping two pieces from her foot, over her shoulder, and back down to her foot.) Put the lid securely back on the can. You and your child have invented "stilts"!

Block Play

Learning opportunities abound in block play.

Block play is perfect for introducing and practicing thinking and problem-solving skills. During block play, your child uses skills such as estimating, predicting, ordering, matching, sorting, and so on. He also uses creativity, eye-hand coordination, and large and small muscle coordination. Encourage your child to play with blocks—for discovery, for learning, and for enjoyment.

Playing with blocks is even more interesting when you and your child invent and construct accessories to use with the blocks. Here are some ideas to get you started.

- Small lumber scraps, such as flat pieces for bridges or roofs.
- Small stones, shells, and sticks to use for "cargo."
- Tile, linoleum, or carpet samples.
- Berry box "cages."
- Craft sticks (can be used to make fences and road signs).
- Easter grass (can be used as hay).
- Small cardboard traffic signs or labels on the buildings your child constructs.
- Dollhouse furniture.
- Junk drawer items such as spools, golf tees, rubber or plastic tubing, small plastic cups, and so on.

Magnets

A few magnets can provide your child with hours of enjoyment and challenges.

Try to have a variety of magnets on hand (your child may find some if she does the "Take-Aparts" activity on page 22). Good ones include horseshoe magnets, bar magnets, donut-shaped magnets, magnet wands, and magnetic marbles. Alphabet magnets and novelty magnets are lots of fun, too. Gather an assortment of items from your "junk" drawer (nails, paper clips, metal nuts, washers, plastic tags, twist ties, clothespins, craft sticks, pencils, and so on).

Let your child experiment to find out which objects can and cannot be picked up by the magnets. Divide a piece of paper in half and let your child place the objects that cannot be picked up with the magnets on one side of the paper, and the objects that can be picked up with the magnets on the other side of the paper.

Let your child take one of the magnets and walk around your home to discover places where the magnets will stick. Will a magnet stick to a wooden shelf? To a tile floor? To a metal table leg? To a metal lamp? Let your child call out the name of any object the magnet will stick to.

More Magnet Fun

Let your child practice more challenging thinking skills with these magnet ideas.

Gather an assortment of magnets, magnetic items, and nonmagnetic items, and try some of the following ideas for using magnets in new and exciting ways.

❋ Have your child place a small magnet in a shallow plastic container. Next, show him how to move a strong magnet under the container to make the small magnet move. For extra fun, place a sheet of white paper in the container and pour in a little paint. Drop in the magnet, and let your child move the strong magnet underneath the container to create a magnet painting.

❋ Place a handful of metal tacks in a plastic jar and screw the lid on tightly. Let your child use a strong magnet to hold the tacks onto the side of the jar. What happens when he removes the magnet? Try using small nails, washers, or metal shavings from a hardware store.

❋ Gather several each of three magnetic objects (paper clips, washers, and small screws), and three nonmagnetic objects (plastic buttons, pebbles, glass marbles). Set out a magnet and a muffin tin, and let your child use the magnet to separate the magnetic items from the nonmagnetic items. Let him sort all of the items into separate piles, and then use the magnet to place the magnetic items into the muffin cups.

My Light

To make this toy, you will need a D battery, a 1-by 6-inch-long piece of aluminum foil, a flashlight bulb, and transparent tape. Tear a 6-inch piece of tape and place it down the middle of the dull side of the aluminum foil (this makes the foil sturdier). Fold the foil in thirds lengthwise, shiny side out. Tape one end of the foil strip to the flat end of the battery and stand the battery on a table. The light bulb is now ready to be lit.

With your child, take a walk around your home and point out all of the different types of lights and light switches you see. Tell your child that you've made a special light just for her. Show her the battery and the light bulb. Help her hold the bulb upright on top of the battery and touch the loose end of the foil strip to the bulb's metal side. Celebrate when the bulb lights up!

Explain that the bulb lights up because electricity is flowing through the battery, the foil, and into the light bulb, just as it flows from the light switches in your home through wires, wall outlets, a light's cord, and into light bulbs.

Your child will want to light her bulb over and over again.

This is sure to become one of your child's favorite science experiences.

Erupting Volcano

Vinegar, sand, and baking soda are all you and your child need to make a volcano erupt!

To make the volcano, let your child help you place some wet sand in a cardboard box and mold it into a volcano shape. Push a small glass into the top of the volcano to make the crater. Fill the glass half full of vinegar and add a few drops of red food coloring. Add 1 tablespoon of baking soda to the vinegar, and then watch the eruption together. Try this experiment with both warm and cold vinegar. Talk to your child about the differences in the eruptions.

Try to find some pictures of real volcanic eruptions. Your librarian can suggest books about volcanoes that may have good pictures, or the library may even have a video about volcanoes. Let your child compare his volcano's eruption with the eruption of a real volcano.

Water and Bubble Fun

Inside or out, children are always busy and happy when they are experimenting with water and bubbles.

Here are some activities to do with water and bubbles. You and your child will be amazed at all of the fun and learning that can happen with water, soap, and a few other simple materials.

⊠ Find some small scraps of crepe paper (the old-fashioned, inexpensive kind that bleeds) and put just an inch or so of water in a clear glass. Ask your child, "What do you think will happen if we put this piece of yellow paper in the water? Will it float?" Let your child try it and see. The paper will float at first, but will sink as it gets wet and heavy. Ask the child what else is happening. Where did that yellow color come from? Point out that the crepe paper has faded since you put it into the water. Now ask your child to try this again with a very small piece of blue paper, and tell you what happens. This is a wonderful way to show your child that blue and yellow make green.

⊠ At a table outdoors or in the house, place several layers of paper towels under individual plastic cups containing an inch of water, a few drops of liquid soap, and a straw. Blow lots of bubbles to overflow the cups. Next, carefully drop a few droplets of food coloring on top of the bubbles. The beautiful geometric designs that appear will amaze you and your child.

⊠ Go outside together and let your child blow some bubbles. Try to have different types of bubble blowers available. Help your child notice that bubbles aren't always round. Some are ovals, and, when they hook together, some are flower-shaped or figure-8-shaped.

⊠ Find a large paintbrush and fill a bucket with water. Take your child outside on a warm day and let her "paint" the side of the house or the driveway with water. Point out how the surface darkens in color. Then check the time and find out how long it takes for the water "paint" to disappear or evaporate.

Beanbag Games

If you don't have a set of beanbags, make some! Simply fill an old sock with 2 or 3 inches of dry rice or beans, tie or sew it closed about an inch above the beans, and cut off the remainder of the sock. Or, sew two fabric pieces together to make a pouch, pour in rice or beans, and sew it closed. By making beanbags yourself, you can use various fabrics and make many different shapes and sizes for your child.

Look around the house or in a fabric store to find brightly colored scrap materials in various textures, such as velvet, fake fur, suede, or satin. Try making your beanbags in heart shapes, triangles, circles, rectangles, or squares. Make some large and small beanbags of the same shape or color.

Try some of the following beanbag games with your child.

Beanbag games can teach colors, shapes, sizes, letters, or numbers.

- Outline some shapes on the floor with masking tape and ask your child to toss a beanbag into the triangle, circle, square, or rectangle.

- Help your child practice the names of parts of the body. Have him walk in a circle with a beanbag on his head, in his elbow, between his knees, on one hip, and so on.

- Use a permanent marker to write a different numeral on each of several empty plastic gallon milk jugs. Line them up on a fence or a bench. Call out a number and let your child toss a beanbag at the bottle with that number written on it.

Shopping

The grocery store is a fantastic environment for practicing thinking skills.

While on a shopping trip with your child, point out the prices posted on the shelves or on the products. Let her help you find the items on your list. Show your child the different sections in the store for each type of product. In the produce section, point out that all of the vegetables are together, but some are in refrigerated shelves and some are not. Can she guess why? You can also point out that some vegetables are frozen and some are canned.

Ask your child to watch for different kinds of potatoes, peppers, carrots, etc. Are all the fruits together? How many different colors and varieties of apples, for example, can your child find? Let her weigh some fruits or vegetables on a produce scale.

Flashlights and Magnifying Glasses

Encourage your child's observation skills with these fun tools.

A small magnifying glass and a mini-flashlight are wonderful tools for creating thinking-skill activities away from home. Give the flashlight or the magnifying glass to your child and encourage him to observe, think, and tell.

In a restaurant, for example, examining a cracker or an ice cube with a flashlight and a magnifying glass is a whole new discovery experience. Encourage your child to tell you all about what he sees.

Riddles

Riddles are lots of fun, and they encourage children to draw upon their past experiences and really think.

When playing riddle games with your child, try to use riddles that describe something she is familiar with. If she seems stuck, give more clues until she solves the riddle. You can use the riddles that follow or try making up some of your own. After your child solves several riddles, encourage her to make up some of her own.

⌗ I am thinking of something red and round that we eat at lunchtime. (Apple)

⌗ I am thinking of something hard that we can string to make necklaces, but when we eat it with cheese it is squishy and soft. (Macaroni)

⌗ What is big and purple and likes to sing and dance? (Barney)

⌗ The sun and bananas are this color. (Yellow)

⌗ I am thinking of something that cries and sleeps a lot. (A baby)

What If?

"What-if" questions help children practice critical thinking, memory, and problem-solving skills.

"What-if" questions require children to imagine problem situations and think about different aspects of a question, or decide upon an action to take. What-ifs can also help you teach values, safety lessons, and other important concepts. The wonderful thing about what-if questions is that they can be used anytime and anyplace. Below are some examples of what-if questions. Be sure to make up some of your own what-if questions, and let your child think of some to ask you, too.

- What if we had to make this trip in a horse and buggy instead of in a car?
- What if our car could float like a boat?
- What if we see a hitch-hiker on the road?
- What if we lost our money?

- What if the only colors in the world were red and yellow?
- What if you were as tiny as an ant?
- What if animals could talk?
- What if we didn't have any beds?
- What if we could only hop and not walk or run?

Title Index

ACTIVITY BOOKS

BEST OF TOTLINE
Totline Magazine's best ideas.
Best of Totline Newsletter
Best of Totline Parent Flyers

BUSY BEES SERIES
Seasonal ideas for twos and threes.
Busy Bees–Fall
Busy Bees–Winter
Busy Bees–Spring
Busy Bees–Summer

CELEBRATION SERIES
Early learning through celebrations.
Small World Celebrations
Special Day Celebrations
Great Big Holiday
   Celebrations
Celebrating Likes
   and Differences

EXPLORING SERIES
Versatile, hands-on learning.
Exploring Sand
Exploring Water
Exploring Wood

FOUR SEASONS
Active learning through the year.
Four Seasons–Art
Four Seasons–Math
Four Seasons–Movement
Four Seasons–Science

GREAT BIG THEMES SERIES
Giant units designed around a theme.
Space • Farm • Zoo • Circus

LEARNING & CARING ABOUT
Teach children about their world.
Our World
Our Selves
Our Town

PIGGYBACK® SONGS
New songs sung to the tunes of childhood favorites!
Piggyback Songs
More Piggyback Songs
Piggyback Songs for
   Infants and Toddlers
Holiday Piggyback Songs
Animal Piggyback Songs
Piggyback Songs for School
Piggyback Songs to Sign
Spanish Piggyback Songs
More Piggyback Songs
   for School

PLAY & LEARN SERIES
Learning through familiar objects.
Play & Learn with Magnets
Play & Learn with
   Rubber Stamps
Play & Learn with Photos
Play & Learn with Stickers
Play & Learn with
   Paper Shapes & Borders

Totline® PUBLICATIONS
The most trusted name in early learning resources

1•2•3 SERIES
Open-ended learning.
1•2•3 Art
1•2•3 Games
1•2•3 Colors
1•2•3 Puppets
1•2•3 Reading & Writing
1•2•3 Rhymes, Stories & Songs
1•2•3 Math
1•2•3 Science
1•2•3 Shapes

THEME-A-SAURUS® SERIES
Classroom-tested, instant themes.
Theme-A-Saurus
Theme-A-Saurus II
Toddler Theme-A-Saurus
Alphabet Theme-A-Saurus
Nursery Rhyme
   Theme-A-Saurus
Storytime Theme-A-Saurus
Multisensory Theme-A-Saurus

PARENT BOOKS

A YEAR OF FUN SERIES
Age-specific books for parenting.
Just for Babies
Just for Ones
Just for Twos
Just for Threes
Just for Fours
Just for Fives

BEGINNING FUN WITH ART
Introduce your child to art fun.
Craft Sticks • Crayons • Felt
Glue • Paint • Paper Shapes
Modeling Dough
Tissue Paper • Scissors
Rubber Stamps • Stickers
Yarn

LEARNING EVERYWHERE
Discover teaching opportunities everywhere you go.
Teaching House
Teaching Trips
Teaching Town

STORYTIME

Delightful stories with related activity ideas, snacks, and songs.

ALPHABET & NUMBER SERIES
Kids Celebrate the Alphabet
Kids Celebrate Numbers

HUFF AND PUFF® SERIES
Huff and Puff's Snowy Day
Huff and Puff
   on Groundhog Day
Huff and Puff's Hat Relay
Huff and Puff's April Showers
Huff and Puff's
   Hawaiian Rainbow
Huff and Puff Go to Camp
Huff and Puff's Fourth of July
Huff and Puff Around
   the World
Huff and Puff Go to School
Huff and Puff on Halloween
Huff and Puff
   on Thanksgiving
Huff and Puff's
   Foggy Christmas

NATURE SERIES
The Bear and the Mountain
Ellie the Evergreen
The Wishing Fish

RESOURCES

BEAR HUGS® SERIES
Encourage positive attitudes.
Remembering the Rules
Staying in Line
Circle Time
Transition Times
Time Out
Saying Goodbye
Meals and Snacks
Nap Time
Cleanup
Fostering Self-Esteem
Being Afraid
Saving the Earth
Being Responsible
Getting Along
Being Healthy
Welcoming Children
Respecting Others
Accepting Change

MIX & MATCH PATTERNS
Simple patterns to save time!
Animal • Everyday
Holiday • Nature

PROBLEM SOLVING SAFARI
Teaching problem solving skills.
Problem Solving—Art
Problem Solving—Blocks
Problem Solving—
   Dramatic Play
Problem Solving—
   Manipulatives
Problem Solving—Outdoors
Problem Solving—Science

101 TIPS FOR DIRECTORS
Valuable tips for busy directors.
Staff and Parent Self-Esteem
Parent Communication
Health and Safety
Marketing Your Center
Resources for You
   and Your Center
Child Development Training

101 TIPS
FOR PRESCHOOL TEACHERS
Valuable tips for teachers.
Creating Theme
   Environments
Encouraging Creativity
Developing Motor Skills
Developing Language Skills
Teaching Basic Concepts
Spicing Up Learning
   Centers

101 TIPS
FOR TODDLER TEACHERS
Valuable tips for teachers.
Classroom Management
Discovery Play
Dramatic Play
Large Motor Play
Small Motor Play
Word Play

1001 SERIES
Super reference books.
1001 Teaching Props
1001 Teaching Tips
1001 Rhymes & Fingerplays

SNACKS SERIES
Nutrition combines with learning.
Super Snacks
Healthy Snacks
Teaching Snacks
Multicultural Snacks

PUZZLES/POSTERS

PUZZLES
Kids Celebrate the Alphabet
Kids Celebrate Numbers
African Adventure
Underwater Adventure
Bear Hugs Health Puzzles
Busy Bees

POSTERS
We Work and Play Together
Bear Hugs Sing-Along
   Health Posters
Busy Bees